REMARKABLE CANADIANS

Robert Bateman

by Carol Koopmans

Published by Weigl Educational Publishers Limited
6325 – 10 Street SE
Calgary, Alberta, Canada
T2H 2Z9

Website: www.weigl.com

Library and Archives Canada Cataloguing in Publication

Koopmans, Carol
        Robert Bateman / Carol Koopmans.

(Remarkable Canadians)
ISBN 978-1-55388-317-3 (bound).--ISBN 978-1-55388-318-0 (pbk.)

                        1. Bateman, Robert, 1930- --Juvenile literature.
2. Painters--Canada--Biography--Juvenile literature.
3. Naturalists--Canada--Biography--Juvenile literature.
I. Title. II. Series.

ND249.B3175K66 2007   j759.11   C2007-900886-0

Printed in the United States of America
1 2 3 4 5 6 7 8 9 0 11 10 09 08 07

Editor: Liz Brown
Design: Terry Paulhus

We acknowledge the financial support of the Government of Canada through the Book
Publishing Industry Development Program (BPIDP) for our publishing activities.

Cover: Robert Bateman is one of Canada's best-known artists.

Photograph Credits:
Cover: Courtesy of Robert Bateman; Courtesy of Robert Bateman: pages 5, 6, 8, 10, 14,
16, 18, 19, 20; Photographed by Birgit Freybe Bateman: pages 9, 17; Photographed by
Norm Lightfoot: page 3; Registered by the Government of Ontario under the Trade
Marks Act: page 7, top left.

Contents

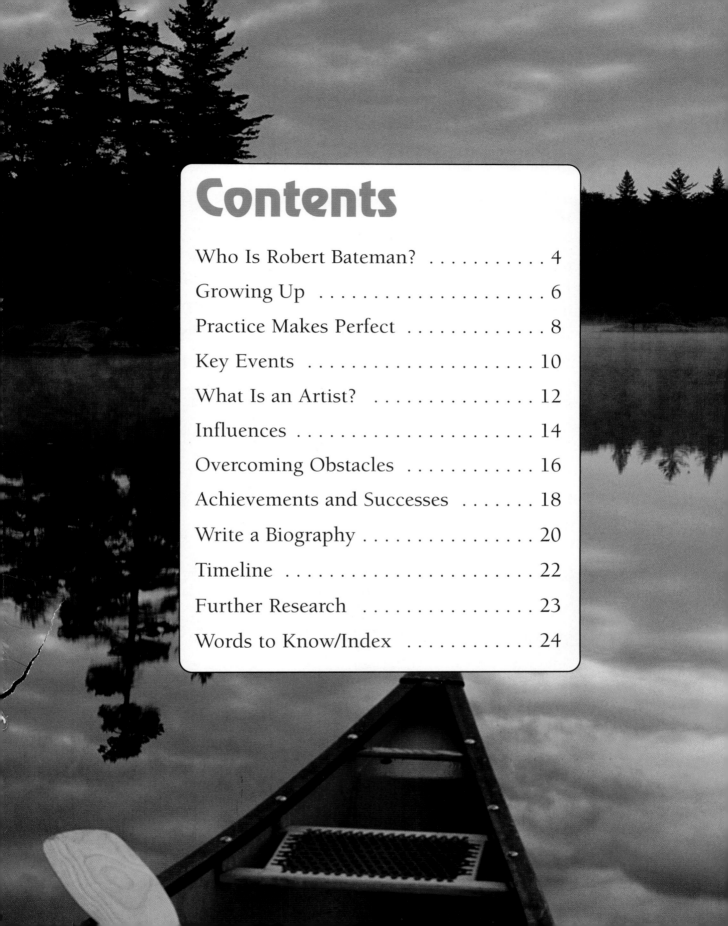

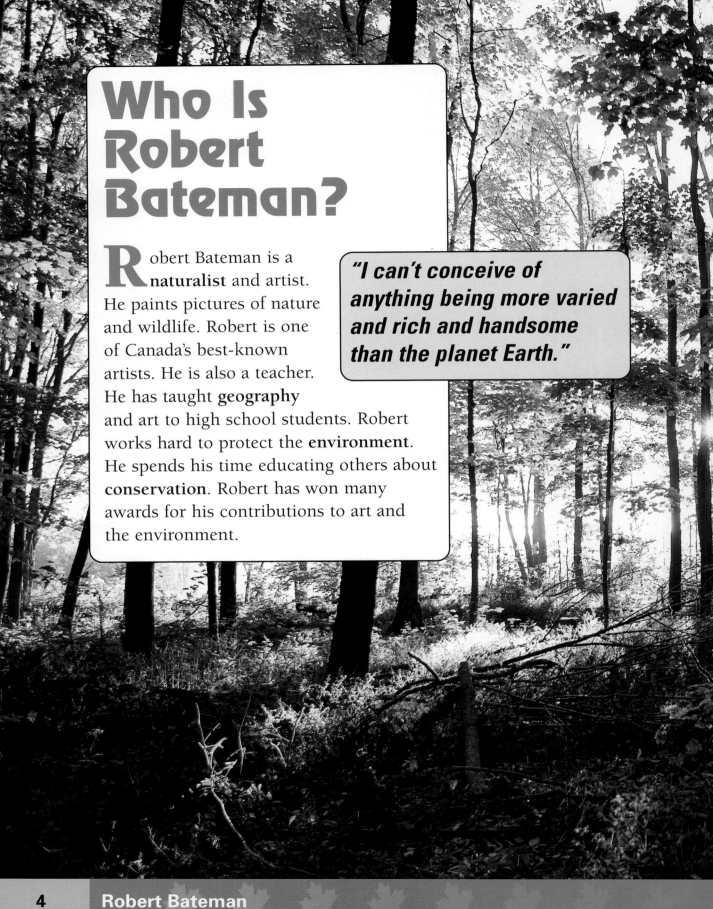

Who Is Robert Bateman?

Robert Bateman is a **naturalist** and artist. He paints pictures of nature and wildlife. Robert is one of Canada's best-known artists. He is also a teacher. He has taught **geography** and art to high school students. Robert works hard to protect the **environment**. He spends his time educating others about **conservation**. Robert has won many awards for his contributions to art and the environment.

"I can't conceive of anything being more varied and rich and handsome than the planet Earth."

Growing Up

On May 24, 1930, Robert McLellan Bateman was born in Toronto, Ontario. Robert's parents were Joseph and Anne Bateman. Robert's father was an electrical engineer. An electrical engineer is a person who creates and fixes electrical systems. Robert has two brothers, Jack and Ross. He is the oldest child in his family.

Growing up, Robert was interested in art and wildlife. In Toronto, he would sketch pictures of the birds that lived around his home. In the summer, Robert's family travelled to their cottage in Haliburton, Ontario. The cottage was close to Algonquin Provincial Park. Algonquin Park is a wildlife sanctuary. This is a place where plants and animals are protected.

🍁 At Algonquin Park, Robert was able to watch and study many animals.

Ontario Tidbits

COAT OF ARMS

BIRD
Common Loon

FLOWER
White Trillium

Toronto is the provincial capital.

Ontario's Algonquin Park is Canada's oldest provincial park.

Lake Superior is the world's largest freshwater lake.

More than 12 million people live in Ontario.

Ontario is the second-largest province in Canada. Quebec is the largest.

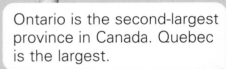

Robert spent his summers near Algonquin Park, Ontario. Find out more about the park. How do you think spending time in Algonquin Park influenced Robert's painting?

Practice Makes Perfect

When Robert was 12, he joined the Junior Field Naturalists Club with his friend, Alan Gordon. The club met on Saturdays at Toronto's Royal Ontario Museum. In the club, Robert and Alan learned about bird **anatomy** and behaviour. They also learned how to carve birds from wood.

While he was a teenager, Robert continued to learn as much as he could about wildlife and nature. At age 17, he took a summer job at Algonquin Park. At this job, Robert learned how to collect wildlife **specimens** and draw pictures of them. When Robert had breaks from work, he would canoe on the lakes in the park and paint pictures.

🍁 When Robert was a teenager, he and his friend Don Smith often went bird-watching.

Robert loved painting. He wanted to be an artist, but he did not think he could earn enough money to support himself. He decided that he would become a teacher. In 1954, Robert earned his degree in geography from the University of Toronto. A year later, he received his teaching certificate from the Ontario College of Education. From 1955 to 1976, he taught high school students art and geography.

🍁 Robert is well known for his paintings, but he is also skilled at other forms of art, such as sculpting.

Key Events

When Robert was 33, he saw an art display by an artist named Andrew Wyeth. This was an important moment for Robert. Wyeth painted pictures exactly the way he saw them in real life. This style of painting is called realism. Robert began painting in this style.

Between 1963 and 1965, Robert took a job teaching geography to students in Nigeria. Nigeria is a country in Africa. Robert painted many pictures of the wildlife there. These pictures were popular with tourists. In Africa, Robert began to realize it might be possible for him to make money as a full-time artist.

When Robert returned to Canada, he continued to teach and paint. In 1975, Robert took time off from teaching to paint pictures for an art show at the Tryon Gallery in London, England. At the show, Robert sold all of his paintings. This convinced him that he could support himself as an artist. In 1976, Robert left teaching to become a full-time artist. Today, Robert uses his paintings to teach people about conservation.

🍁 Robert has said that working in Nigeria was the most demanding and interesting part of his teaching career.

Thoughts from Robert

Robert has always loved art, teaching, and nature. Here are some of the things he has said about his interests.

Robert talks about studying the environment.

"Caring begins with knowing."

Robert talks about his love for painting.

"I squeezed painting into every time space and spilled it over onto other things."

As a child, Robert knows he wants to be an artist.

"I knew by the time I was twelve that I was going to spend a lot of my life doing art and a lot of it looking at birds."

Robert describes his work as an artist.

"Art has to do with **inspiration**, creativity, and skill."

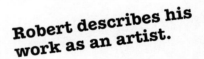

Robert helps protect the environment through his paintings.

"For me, the **preservation** and celebration of the natural world are the underlying motives for...all of my art."

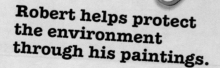

Robert talks about teaching high school students.

"I loved it. I loved preparing for classes, communicating, I loved the mentality of students."

What Is an Artist?

Artists create art in many different ways. Some, such as Robert, use pencils and paints to create pictures. Others create sculptures out of clay. Some artists take pictures with a camera. Artists, such as Robert, make their living by creating and selling works of art. Others enjoy art as a hobby.

Painting can be done anywhere. Many artists paint in a room or building called a studio. Some choose to work outdoors. Sometimes, Robert likes to work outdoors. In addition to sketching and making outlines or models, Robert takes photos. He uses them to help him remember the details of what he observes.

🍁 In cities such as Paris, France, artists often sell their artwork on the street.

Artists 101

A.Y. Jackson (1882–1974)

Type of Artist Painter
Achievements A.Y. Jackson is considered one of the leaders of the **Group of Seven**. Jackson was one of the first artists to paint pictures of Canada. Before Jackson began painting, not many people were interested in Canadian art. Everyone wanted paintings from Europe. Jackson showed people that interesting pictures could be painted in Canada.
Awards Canada Council Medal, 1962; Companion of the Order of Canada, 1968.

Emily Carr (1871–1945)

Type of Artist Painter
Achievements Emily Carr spent most of her life painting pictures of **Aboriginal** culture and Canadian landscapes. Early in Carr's career, people did not value her art. Today, many people around the world enjoy looking at Carr's art. Carr wrote books as well. Her first book was called *Klee Wyck*. It was a collection of stories about Carr's visits to Aboriginal villages.
Awards Governor General's Literary Award, 1941.

Michael Dumas (1950–)

Type of Artist Painter
Achievements Michael Dumas paints wildlife. He uses his paintings to raise money and educate other people about animals that are **endangered**. Dumas' paintings have appeared on Canadian coins and postage stamps. His paintings have been displayed in many places, including Great Britain and Japan.
Awards Master Palette Award, 2005; Peterborough Pathway of Fame, 2004.

Carl Schaefer (1903–1995)

Type of Artist Painter and Illustrator
Achievements Carl Schaefer is best known for his paintings of the southern Ontario landscape. In 1943, he was **commissioned** to paint pictures for the Royal Canadian Air Force. Many of Schaefer's paintings are now on display at the Canadian War Museum in Ottawa.
Awards Guggenheim Fellowship, 1940; Queen's Medal, 1953; Canada Centennial Medal, 1967; Member of the Order of Canada, 1978.

The Paintbrush
Artists use many kinds of tools to help them do their work. Each kind of art has its own set of tools. A paintbrush is one tool used by artists who paint. Artists choose paintbrushes based on their painting styles. There are many different shapes of paintbrushes to choose from, such as round, flat, and mop.

Influences

Many artists and wildlife experts influenced Robert's career. At the Royal Ontario Museum, Robert met two artists who helped him develop his skills. Frank Smith was a wood carver. He taught Robert how to carve birds and make bird models from plasticine. Terence Shortt was an expert on birds and a skilled painter. He taught Robert about birds and how to paint pictures.

When Robert was a teenager, he became interested in the paintings of other Canadian artists. He admired the artists in the Group of Seven. He also admired the paintings of Emily Carr. The painting styles of these artists influenced Robert's own style.

Robert Bateman has used his knowledge of birds to help protect them. He was an honourary chairman of the Return of the Peregrine Falcon Project. This is a project to bring back peregrine falcons to the Okanagan Valley in British Columbia.

When Robert was 18, he began taking painting lessons from Gordon Payne. Gordon was a well-known artist. For two years, Robert took painting classes with Gordon. He showed Robert new painting skills. Gordon taught Robert about other well-known artists, such as Pablo Picasso.

In 1950, Robert began taking drawing classes from Carl Schaefer. Carl was an artist who had worked with the Group of Seven. He taught Robert a new method for drawing. Robert practised this method for five years, until he could do it quickly. These lessons and the lessons at the Royal Ontario Museum improved Robert's skills as an artist.

The Royal Ontario Museum

The Royal Ontario Museum (ROM) opened in 1914. It is located near Queen's Park, in Toronto. The ROM is the fifth-largest museum in North America. It has the largest **field research** department in Canada. To see some of the different activities the ROM has for kids, visit http://www.rom.on.ca/schools/rom_kids

🍁 Many students visit the ROM for school trips and special activities.

Overcoming Obstacles

Robert faced obstacles as an artist. Despite this, he has had a successful career. When Robert became a well-known artist, many people wanted his paintings. He could not paint enough pictures for everyone who wanted to own them. In 1977, Mill Pond Press decided to make **reproduction prints** of Robert's paintings. Some people were upset by this. These people thought that original paintings and prints were special and should not be copied.

Robert often travels to different parts of Canada and the world to teach people about protecting wildlife and the environment. He must attend meetings and special events. Today, Robert's biggest obstacle is finding time to paint. Many people want to meet Robert and hear him speak about the environment and his art.

Robert signs each of his reproduction prints to make sure that they are of high quality.

Robert paints for most of the day when he is at home. He has had to learn to paint with many distractions. He often continues painting when visitors come to see him. Each year, Robert completes 8 to 12 large paintings. He also paints many smaller ones.

Painting is hard work for Robert. It is challenging for him to create good paintings. However, Robert enjoys his job. He has said that, as long as he is able to hold a brush, he will continue to paint.

🍁 Robert sometimes talks on the phone while he paints.

Achievements and Successes

Robert has had much success in his career. Many people around the world want to see his paintings. Robert has presented many major displays of his work in places such as Great Britain, the United States, Japan, and South Africa.

Robert's paintings hang on the walls of many museums and people's homes. In 1981, the Canadian government asked Robert to create a special painting. This painting was a wedding gift for Charles, the Prince of Wales, and Lady Diana Spencer.

🍁 In 1993, Robert painted a picture of himself standing next to an ancient tree that had just been cut down. This painting drew attention to the logging of the Carmanah rain forest in British Columbia, where 800-year-old trees were being cut down.

Through his painting, Robert has made many more people aware of the Canadian wilderness. Robert was made an Officer of the Order of Canada in 1984. This award recognizes a lifetime of service to Canada. Robert received this award in recognition of his art and the work he has done to protect the environment.

Robert has won many awards for his work in conservation. In 1998, the United States National Audubon Society honoured Robert as one of the 20th Century's 100 Champions of Conservation. Robert believes it is important to teach people about conservation. In 2010, he will help open The Robert Bateman Art and Environmental Education Centre in Victoria, British Columbia.

The Robert Bateman Art and Environmental Education Centre

The Robert Bateman Art and Environmental Education Centre will be located at Royal Roads University in Victoria, British Columbia. Many of Robert's paintings will be on display. Robert has donated some of his sketchbooks and letters. Visitors will be able to look at them when they come to the centre. Robert will give lectures to help people understand wildlife.

Royal Roads University opened in 1995.

Write a Biography

A person's life story can be the subject of a book. This kind of book is called a biography. Biographies describe the lives of remarkable people, such as those who have achieved great success or have done important things to help others. These people may be alive today, or they may have lived many years ago. Reading a biography can help you learn more about a remarkable person.

At school, you might be asked to write a biography. First, decide who you want to write about. You can choose an artist, such as Robert Bateman, or any other person you find interesting. Then, find out if your library has any books about this person. Learn as much as you can about him or her. Write down the key events in this person's life. What was this person's childhood like? What has he or she accomplished? What are his or her goals? What makes this person special or unusual?

A concept web is a useful research tool. Read the questions in the following concept web. Answer the questions in your notebook. Your answers will help you write your biography.

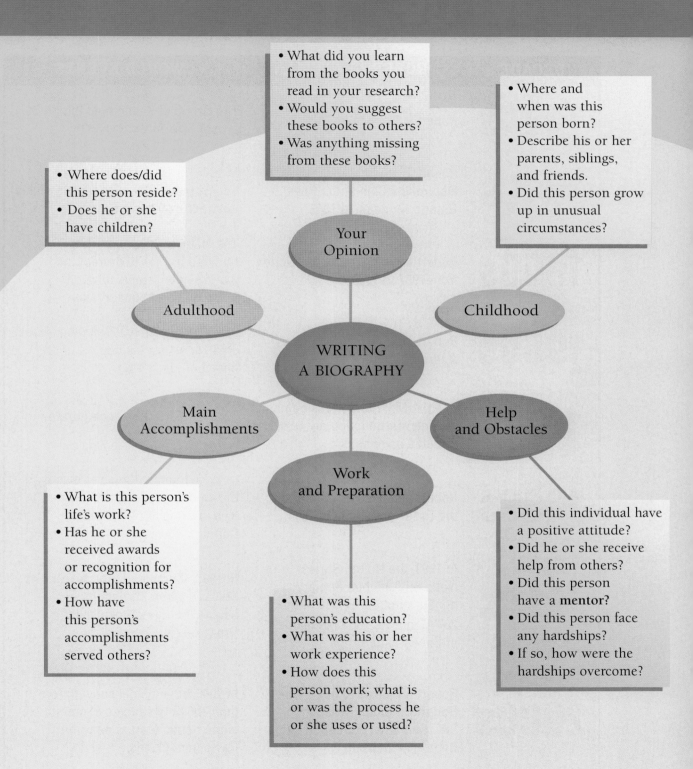

- What did you learn from the books you read in your research?
- Would you suggest these books to others?
- Was anything missing from these books?

- Where and when was this person born?
- Describe his or her parents, siblings, and friends.
- Did this person grow up in unusual circumstances?

- Where does/did this person reside?
- Does he or she have children?

Your Opinion

Adulthood

Childhood

WRITING A BIOGRAPHY

Main Accomplishments

Help and Obstacles

Work and Preparation

- What is this person's life's work?
- Has he or she received awards or recognition for accomplishments?
- How have this person's accomplishments served others?

- What was this person's education?
- What was his or her work experience?
- How does this person work; what is or was the process he or she uses or used?

- Did this individual have a positive attitude?
- Did he or she receive help from others?
- Did this person have a **mentor**?
- Did this person face any hardships?
- If so, how were the hardships overcome?

Timeline

DECADE	ROBERT BATEMAN	WORLD EVENTS
1930s	Robert is born on May 24, 1930.	The Group of Seven hold their first art show in Toronto in 1931.
1940s	Robert joins the Junior Field Naturalists Club at the Royal Ontario Museum in 1942.	In 1946, artist Jackson Pollock begins painting in a new style called **abstract expressionism**.
1950s	Robert travels around the world from 1957 to 1958.	The Nature Conservancy is founded in 1951 to protect the world's **ecosystems** through environmental conservation.
1960s	Robert views an art exhibit by Andrew Wyeth in 1962.	In the 1960s, Andy Warhol becomes well known for his pop art or art based on the media.
1970s	In 1977, Mill Pond Press begins making reproduction prints of Robert's paintings.	The first Earth Day is celebrated in 1970.
1980s	Robert becomes an Officer of the Order of Canada in 1984.	In 1988, Randy Stoltmann discovers the world's tallest Sitka spruce tree in British Columbia's Carmanah valley.
1990s	In 1998, the United States National Audubon Society honours Robert as one of the 20th Century's 100 Champions of Conservation.	In 1997, Canada and the United States sign an agreement to begin clean-up of toxins in the Great Lakes.
2000s	Robert prepares to open The Robert Bateman Art and Environmental Education Centre, in Victoria.	In 2006, scientists discover more than 100 new species of marine life in the ocean waters near the Hawai'ian Islands.

Further Research

How can I find out more about Robert Bateman?

Most libraries have computers that connect to a database for researching information. If you input a key word, you will be provided with a list of books in the library that contain information on that topic. Non-fiction books are arranged numerically, using their call number. Fiction books are organized alphabetically by the author's last name.

Websites

To learn more about Robert Bateman, visit www.robertbateman.ca

To learn more about wildlife, visit www.gettoknow.ca

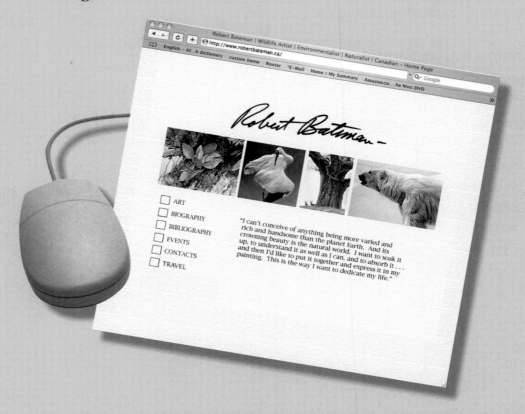

Words to Know

aboriginal: culture of the people who lived in North America before the arrival of Europeans

abstract expressionism: large paintings created by pouring paint on a canvas

anatomy: knowledge of human or animal bodies and how they work

commissioned: given an order for a work of art

conservation: protecting the environment

ecosystems: communities of plants and animals

endangered: at risk of dying out

environment: the natural world

field research: studies done outside

geography: the study of Earth's surface

Group of Seven: a group of seven artists who worked and travelled together painting nature and landscapes in Canada

inspiration: encouragement to create a work of art

mentor: a wise and trusted teacher

naturalist: a person who studies plants and animals

preservation: the act of keeping something in its original state

reproduction prints: copies that are made of an original painting

specimens: animals used as examples for scientific study

Index